MW00886593

101 Coolest Things to

Do in China

Introduction

So you're going to China, huh? You lucky lucky thing! You are sure in for a treat because China is truly one of the most magical countries on this planet.

Around the country, from the cities the countryside, you will find epic landscapes, some of the greatest food you'll ever put in your mouth, history that extends backwards for centuries, incredible festivities, and loads of parties to boot.

In this guide, we'll be giving you the low down on:
- the very best things to shove in your pie hole, from street food on the streets of Shanghai to incredible restaurants where you can enjoy a romantic meal for two
- the best shopping so that you can take a little piece of China back home with you, whether that's in the form of some incredible Chinese porcelain or ingredients for cooking your own incredible Chinese dishes
- incredible festivals, whether you want to celebrate Chinese New Year with local people or you would prefer to rock out to Chinese rock bands in the Chinese grasslands
- the coolest historical and cultural sights that you simply cannot afford to miss from ancient Buddhist temples through to caves with ancient art work

- the best places to have a few glasses of rice wine and party like a local
- and tonnes more coolness besides!

Let's not waste any more time – here are the 101 coolest things not to miss in China!

1. Take a Stroll Along the Great Wall of China

Without a doubt, the Great Wall of China is one of the most iconic sights on the face of the planet. While the rumours that the wall can be seen from space are unfounded, it's still gargantuan and incredibly impressive when you are up close to it. And if you really want to have an incredible adventure that you will remember forever, you can take one of the many hikes that run along the course of the Great Wall. As it snakes its way across China for 20,000 kilometres, you might just want to pick one section!

2. Visit the Famous Statues of the Terracotta Army

If you want to discover a part of China's ancient history, you absolutely cannot miss a trip to the Terracotta Army located in the Xi'an region of the country. The Terracotta Army is essentially a collection of terracotta military sculptures, such as soldiers, chariots, horses, and more besides. Quite unbelievably, these sculptures date back to the 3rd century, and they were buried with the emperor at the time to protect the emperor in his afterlife.

3. Get Really Close to Tigers at the Siberian Tiger Park

Siberian tigers are among the most beautiful animals in the world, but sadly there are only about 500 of these big cats left in the wild. Without places like the Siberian Tiger Park in Harbin, whose conservation efforts help to repopulate the species, the Siberian Tigers would be extinct. A trip to this park is nothing short of a magical experience for animal lovers. You have the opportunity to get really close to the tigers through a fence, and ride a vehicle through the fields that the tigers will often chase.

4. Walk Through the Forbidden City

For any history buff visiting China, the Forbidden City is one of the most important historic sites that you simply need to visit. Quite amazingly, the Forbidden City is the largest palace complex in the whole world, and it's the most expansive and best preserved collection of ancient buildings in China. This palace complex was the Imperial Palace throughout the Ming Dynasty, from 1420 until 1912. You'll see an incredible range of architecture and art as you walk around, and it can be great to take a tour through the complex to really get to grips with everything on display.

5. Have Clothes Made at the South Bund Fabric Market

If you fancy yourself as something of a fashionista and you would like to take back some killer threads with you, skip the high street shops and head to the far more exciting South Bund Fabric Market instead. This market is located in Shanghai, is open daily, and is home to hundreds of tailors and seamstresses. You simply pick out your fabric, have your measurements taken, and pick a style, and within a couple of days you'll have clothes that have been made just for you. Don't be scared to haggle – it's a part of the local market culture

6. Tuck Into an Authentic Sichuan Hot Pot

On a trip to China, your idea of Chinese food will be totally flipped on its head, and if you like your food spicy, you need to make sure that you travel to the Sichuan region, where the local people like their food packed with spice and heat. In this region, Sichuan Hot Pot is by far the most famous and most delicious dish. As the name would suggest, this is a simmering pot full of ingredients, and the most important ingredient of them all is the fiery hot Sichuan pepper.

7. Say Hi to Giant Pandas in Chengdu

One of the cutest and most majestic animals native to China is the giant panda. As beautiful as these creatures are, they are sadly endangered, and reliant on conservation to keep them alive. The Chengdu Research Base of Giant Panda Breeding started with 6 pandas in 1987, and now has more than 120. It is possible to take a 3 hour tour of the facility, learn about all of their great work, and get really close to these truly stunning creatures. And your entrance fee will go towards furthering the incredible work of the research base.

8. Take in a Peking Opera Show

After a day of museum hopping and strolling around in Beijing, what are some of the fun things that you can do in the evening time? Well, one of our favourite things is to take in a traditional Peking Opera show. This is not like the kind opera that you would experience at home, and it combines mime, singing, vocal performance, dance, acrobatics, and the most spectacular costumes. Liyuan Theatre in Beijing is the probably the best place to take in one of these shows.

9. Discover an Incredible Collection of Buddhist Art

The religious and spiritual practice of Buddhism has a long and illustrious history throughout China, and this is evident in many sites around the country. One of the most important sites of Buddhist history in the country is the Mogao Caves. This system of Buddhist cave temples was active from the 4th to the 14th centuries., and there are about 600 cave temples that have survived. In these caves, you can see some of the most incredible cave art that exists anywhere on the planet.

10. Top Up Your Tan at Yalong Bay

When you think of incredible beach destinations in Asia, your mind will probably first wander to the islands of Thailand or the Philippines, and while those certainly are spectacular beach destinations, you absolutely shouldn't discount China for a spot of beach action. There are also islands away from mainland China, and Hainan is almost certainly the most beautiful of them all. In fact, Hainan is often nicknamed the Hawaii of China, and it's with good reason. The sand is soft, the sea is blue, and Yalong Bay is the best beach on the island.

11. Hike Through the Yading Nature Reserve

China is a country of epic contrasts. You will find bustling cities such as Beijing and Shanghai, but also vast expanses of nature where you won't see buildings for hundreds of miles. If you are someone who wants to explore the natural beauty of China, the Yading Nature Reserve should absolutely be on your hit list. This is the ultimate place in China for hiking. Inside the reserve, you can discover beautiful trickling rivers, rocky areas, grasslands, and mountains besides.

12. Go Dumpling Crazy at Mr Shi's Dumplings

Beijing is a city that seems to have been made with foodies in mind. On every street you'll find street vendors, small local restaurants, and fancy places to eat too. So much choice can be overwhelming, but we're going to make it so much easier for you by telling you that you absolutely need to make at least one stop for lunch at Mr Shi's Dumplings. As the name would suggest, all that's served up are dumplings, either with pork, vegetables, or shrimp inside. They are cheap and incredibly moreish.

13. Have a Day of Learning at the National Museum of China

Considering that China is such a gigantic country, and that it also boats an incredible history in virtually every respect, the museums in the country don't really show off the country in the way that they should. The National Museum of China is an exception, and it's a must-visit while in Beijing. In fact, it's well worth spending a few days in the museum because the collection is staggering. There's more than 1 million items, that cover history from 1.7 million years ago, right up to the end of the Qing dynasty.

14. Try the Street Yoghurts of Beijing

As you walk along the streets of Beijing, your senses will be overloaded by all the different types of food on offer on the streets. One food that you'll no doubt notice again and again is yoghurt served in small glass jars. Although you wouldn't think of yoghurt as being typically Chinese, these are hugely popular in Beijing. The yoghurt is drunk there and then on the street and the glass is then returned to the street stall. It's thick like a milkshake but much tangier. Ultra delicious.

15. Cycle Around the Thousand Island Lake

The Thousand Island Lake is one of the areas of incredible beauty in China. The lake is huge, and unsurprisingly, it has been given its name because of the one thousand islands that float on the lake's waters. Cycling around the lake is one of the best ways to take in all of the beauty of the area, and it's especially pleasant to do so during the spring months. As well as seeing incredible nature, you'll also cycle through ancient towns and have the opportunity to see how local people live.

16. Sip on Tea at Maliandao Tea Market

It is no secret that the Chinese love their tea, and indeed, much of the tea that we drink in the West is actually grown in the tea plantations of China. This makes China an extra special place to go tea shopping, and the ultimate place for this is Maliandao Tea Market in Beijing. As well as many varieties of tea, you can find teacups, tea saucers, tea sets, and other beautiful porcelain items that you wouldn't find at home.

17. Eat Dinner on the 91st Floor of the Shanghai World Financial Centre

There's certainly no shortage of incredible dining opportunities throughout China, but one of the most special would have to be dinner at the Dining Room of the Park Hyatt in Shanghai. The reason why dining here is something extra special is because the restaurant is located on the 91st floor of the Shanghai World Financial Centre, and as you eat, you will have the most spectacular view of the whole city illuminated at night.

18. Take in a Show at the National Centre for Performing Arts

After strolling the streets of Beijing all day, you no doubt want to relax and have some fun when it comes to the evening time, and we think one of the best options for an unforgettable Beijing evening it to take in a show at the National Centre for Performing Arts. This totally spectacular and futuristic looking theatre has a titanium dome, and stages performances such as opera shows, ballets, dances, symphony concerts, and more besides. Be sure to keep up to date with their programme!

19. Visit the World's Oldest and Tallest Wooden Pagoda

The Pagoda of Fagong Temple, otherwise known as Muta, is an example of the beauty of Chinese temple architecture as well as its resilience, because this sturdy temple is made from wood and yet it has survived many earthquakes throughout the centuries. This wooden pagoda was built in 1056, and it stands tall at a height of 67.31 metres, which makes it both the tallest and the oldest wooden pagoda in all of China. There's also many stunning Buddhist statues inside the pagoda.

20. Be Wowed by the Jiayuguan Fortress

When you think of majestic fortresses around the world, you might think of India or Europe, but China has its fair share as well. The Jiayuagan Fortress is all the more impressive because of its totally barren surroundings from which this gargantuan structure emerges. There are incredible watchtowers on each corner, that you can imagine would have been incredible lookouts on the Jiayu Pass centuries ago. This is a must visit for military history fanatics.

21. Be Mesmerised by the Dragon Boat Festival

The Chinese love to celebrate, and there are tonnes and tonnes of festivals throughout the year when you are very welcome to join in with the celebrations. In our opinion, the Dragon Boat Festival, is one of the most fun, colourful, and dynamic of them all. This holiday has been observed annually for over 2000 years to commemorate Qu Yuan, an ancient Chinese poet. Dragon boat racing and eating zongzi (sticky bundles of rice) are the customs of the festival, and it is held in June each year.

22. Chow Down on Steamed Chinese Buns

One of the most quintessential Chinese foods that you should eat as much of as you can on your trip is the humble steamed bun, otherwise known as baozi in China. While much of Chinese food is regional, the good news is that you'll pretty much be able to find these wherever you are in the country. Of course, as the Chinese capital, Beijing is the place to find anything and everything, and for our money, the best place for a fluffy steamed bun filled with meat is always from simple street carts in the capital.

23. Celebrate Chinese New Year With Spring Festival

Chinese New Year is a huge deal. Like, such a huge deal that virtually everyone takes a week off work to celebrate, and this means that February is a wonderful time to be in the country. This time of the year is otherwise known as Spring Festival, and it has roots that go back for an astonishing 4000 years. There will be incredible celebrations no matter where you find yourself in the country, and some of the traditions include giving money in red envelopes, eating dumplings, and simply spending time with family.

24. Have an Artsy Day at the National Art Museum of China

Considering that China has such a vibrant and historic arts culture, it can be hard to find galleries sometimes. But if you want a day of total art immersion, fear not, because the National Art Museum of China in Beijing is waiting to be visited. This is one of the largest art museums in all of China, and visiting this gallery is a great way of exploring a huge expanse of Chinese art, because you can find everything from ancient Chinese sculpture to contemporary abstract works inside.

25. Visit the Largest Waterfalls in China

The sight of an incredible, gushing waterfall is one of the most stunning things of the world, and there are plenty of impressive waterfalls right over China. The most impressive of them all, however, simply has to be Huangguosho Waterfall, the largest waterfall in the whole country – actually, in all of Asia! There are easily accessible viewpoints from the waterfall from the front, back, left, right, above, and below.

26. Watch a Show at the Shanghai Grand Theatre

If you find yourself in the city of Shanghai without something to do in the evening time, it can be a great idea to take in a performance at the beyond incredible Shanghai Grand Theatre. The theatre is so beautiful that it functions as a tourist attraction as a piece of architecture alone, but the shows you can see inside are just as enticing. You can find anything from European symphonies to traditional Chinese operas, and many other types of performance besides.

27. Enjoy an Authentic Chinese BBQ in Xi'an

If you are on the hunt for comfort food, you are in the right place, because China is a country that has comfort food in spades, and what could be more comforting than a good old fashioned barbecue? While barbecue is something that you can find right across the country, we think that it's particularly great in the Xi'an, where there are tonnes of restaurants dedicated to grilled meats. It's here that you'll also find delicious lamb, which is not so popular in other parts of the country.

28. Chill Out at Chengde Mountain Resort

If you are visiting China in the summertime and you feel like cooling down, the small city of Chengde is a great place to visit. The Chengde Mountain Resort is essentially an assortment of imperial palaces, gardens, and lakes that were constructed during the Qing Dynasty during the 18th century, and they take up about half of Chengde City. Up there in the mountains, it's much cooler, and a lovely place to spend a week or two, surrounded by opulent gardens, tranquil waters, and incredible palace architecture.

29. Eat at the Lanzhou Night Market

Almost as soon as you arrive in China, you will discover that the local people absolutely love a market, and a night market even more. These are places to socialise with friends, enjoy the summer weather, eat some wonderful street food, and make other purchases. One of our favourite night markets in the country is the Lanzhou Night Market. This is a great place to have a truly local experience, meet some local Chinese people, and share a meal and a few drinks on the street.

30. Play Beach Volleyball on Changli Golden Beach

Although China might not be the country that you associate most strongly with lazy beach days and swimming in the clear ocean, there are a handful of beaches worth visiting in China if you just cannot resist sunshine, sand and ocean. Changli Golden Beach in the Hebei Province is a beach with soft sands that are very clean, and waters that are very swimmable. And if you fancy a more active beach break, there are volleyball courts on the beach too.

31. Go Wild at the Zhangbei Grasslands InMusic Festival

While China can't exactly be thought of as a mecca for music festivals, there are a handful of festivals worth exploring and one of the best has to be the Zhangbei Grasslands InMusic Festival. The festival features DJs and music talent from around the country, but the really great thing about this particular festival is that it's located at least 7 hours away from any major city so it offers a chance to let loose in the countryside.

32. Start Your Day With a Bowl of Congee

As the saying goes, breakfast is the most important meal of the day, and never is this statement truer than when you are travelling and you need fuel for all the sightseeing you'll be doing in China. If you really want to have breakfast like a local, skip the buttered toast and opt for a steaming bowl of congee instead. Congee is essentially a porridge made from rice, but instead of eating it with fruit and honey as you would at home, congee is served up with ingredients such as chicken, pork, and pickled vegetables.

33. Celebrate the Torch Festival in Lijiang

If you want to discover the real China, you have to escape the big cities for a little while, and discover how the minorities around the country choose to live. Within the minority communities of Sichuan and Yunnan, rituals and festivities are very important, and one of the most important celebrations of the year is the Torch Festival. This takes place in July or August each year, and as well as torches being lit to drive out evil spirits, you can experience bull fighting, cock fighting, live performances, and lots of eating and drinking.

34. Try the Chinese Burrito: Erkuai

Of course, everybody knows that the burrito is a type of Mexican food. If you are hankering for a burrito while in China but don't want to go to an overpriced and touristy Mexican restaurant in one of the cities, you might be pleased to learn that China actually has its own variation of a burrito called erkuai. This yummy snack is native to the Yunnan region, and can be hard to find in other parts of the country. Inside, you'll find rice, Sichuan peppers, vegetables, and other treats besides.

35. Visit the Ancient Village of Hongcun

China is a country with incredible amounts of history, and to experience this history, you don't need to walk through the aisles of stuffy museums. In fact, you can best appreciate the history and culture of the country by taking to the streets. One of the best villages to visit for a taste of China in centuries gone by is Hongcun in the Huizhou region. It's here that you can find some of the most celebrated architecture from the Qing and Ming dynasties, and you are even welcome to walk through some of the houses.

36. Drift Along the Nine Bend River

Because China is such a huge country, there is ample space to enjoy peaceful days in nature, and one of the landscapes that we really love is along the Nine Bend River. This river is located in a remote village called Xincun Village in the Wuyi Mountains, so a visit here is really an opportunity to escape the stresses of everyday life. One of the loveliest things to do is to take a raft tour, which will take you slowly along the river, so you can really absorb the surrounding landscapes.

37. Try Roujiamo, the Chinese Hamburger

Chinese food is flavoursome and fantastic, but let's face it, there are times when all you want to do is chow down on a meaty, juicy burger. Right? Well, the good news is that China has its very own variation of the humble hamburger called roujiamo. This is a street food that is most commonly found in the country's Shannxi province, and the basic idea is that minced meat is mixed up with tonnes of spices and that is then sandwiched between slices of mo, a local type of bread.

38. Visit the Longqing Gorge Ice & Snow Festival

Many people avoid China in the winter months for fear of the bitingly cold winter weather, but in all honesty we think that the wintertime is when the country looks at its most beautiful. If you happen to be in China in the winter, the Longqing Gorge Ice & Snow Festival also makes for a great day trip. From mid January to mid February, you can find a stunning array of ice sculptures in Longqing, with each year centring around a different theme. You'll also find ethnic dancing, fireworks shows, and music performances.

39. Ride a Camel on Sand Dunes in Gansu

When you think of China, you probably don't think of desert landscapes, but China is such an expansive country that you can even find a desert oasis there. In the Gansu region, you can find incredible expanses of desert with nothing but gorgeous red sand for miles and miles. There is also an area with undulating sand dunes, and while these are great to look at, you can have an even more immersive experience by taking a camel ride tour over the dunes.

40. Discover Tibetan Culture in Shangrila

Unfortunately, it can be really quite difficult to get permission from the Chinese authorities to enter Tibet on a tourist trip, but if you don't manage to secure permission, fear not because you can still discover some traditional Tibetan culture in the town of Shangrila in the Yunnan province. In the old town, you can visit a few temples, and there is also surrounding countryside that you can explore either on foot or with a rented bicycle.

41. Eat Delicious Ginger Candy in Fenghuang

One of the lovely things about China is that as you travel from region to region, the food and drinks sold on the street will totally change. When you are in Fenghuang, a beautiful town in the Hunan province, you will find a sweet being sold on the street that the locals go crazy for – ginger candy. These ginger sweets are all freshly made, and you can actually see people pulling the candy on the street. The mix of fiery and sweet is something totally irresistible.

42. Bargain Hard in Beijing's Silk Market

The quality of Chinese silk is second to none, and if you play your cards right, you can take some beautiful silk home with you at a fraction of the price that you would ordinarily pay. The key thing is to avoid the tourist shops and head to the Beijing Silk Market instead. There are so many sellers with incredible silks that there is plenty to choose from, and because the competition is high, it means you should absolutely shop around to get the best price matched with incredible quality.

43. Get Back to Nature in Wulingyuan

If you want to completely immerse yourself in nature on your trip to China, you absolutely need to know about the Wulingyuan Scenic Area, a UNESCO Heritage Site that comprises several national parks in the same area. Of course, the amount of space in the parks is incredible, but one of the nicest ways to see the area is by taking the cable cars that exist in the parks. They can take you to otherwise inaccessible lookout points in the mountains where you will find yourself in the clouds.

44. Eat the Best Duck Pancakes of Your Life at Duck de Chine

One of the quintessential Chinese dishes that you have no doubt tried before travelling to China is Peking Duck. The beautiful slices of duck wrapped in thin pancakes and served with hoisin sauce are delicious, but they are extra special in the Duck de Chine restaurant in Beijing. The centre of the meat is always moist and succulent but the exterior is crisped up so that you can experience a taste and texture sensation in every mouthful.

45. Visit a Stunning Orthodox Church in Harbin

As you travel around China, you will, of course, spot more than a couple of temples. While churches are a far less common sight, there is some truly stunning church architecture to be discovered around the country. One of the most beautiful churches is called Saint Sofia Cathedral in a small city called Harbin. The church was built following the construction of the trans-Siberian railway, when there were 100,000 Russian people living in the city of Harbin. Looking at the church, you could be forgiven for thinking you are in St Petersburg.

46. Start Your Day With a "Ci Fan" Rice Ball

Everybody knows that the Chinese love to eat rice, but eating rice is not simply limited to having a bowl of rice as an accompaniment to your main meal. Rice is actually used in many ways, and something that we are particularly fond of in Shanghai is called Ci Fan, which are basically rice balls. If you have ever tried the Japanese onigiri, this is the Chinese equivalent. Tightly packed sticky rice is filled with ingredients such as mustard tubers or pork floss.

47. Take a Cruise Through the Three Gorges

China is a country that is positively bursting full of natural beauty, and one of the most beautiful places you are likely to encounter is the Three Gorges. The Three gorges are three adjacent gorges that are located in the middle of the Yangtze river and have long been renowned for their natural beauty. The Three Gorges takes up a space of around 200 kilometres, so the best way to take in all of the beauty is by taking a relaxing cruise along the river.

48. Enjoy a Night of Cocktails at Ala House

After a long day of sightseeing, what could be more appealing than kicking back in a great atmosphere with a cocktail or two? Well there is certainly no shortage of beautiful cocktail bars in Beijing, but our favourite of them all might just be Ala House. With room for less than thirty people, this is very much a neighbourhood joint where you will feel instantly at home. The staff are friendly and speak English, they serve up classic cocktails, and the prices are very reasonable.

49. Visit China's Oldest Water Town

Zhouzhuang is otherwise known as the Venice of the East, because this ancient village is China's oldest water town. The ancient town has a history that extends back in time for more than 900 years, and it still retains the look and feel of those times gone by. It is possible to take a canal tour on small boats while the people on the boats sing traditional songs to you – a beautiful way of exploring a beautiful part of China.

50. Try a Strange Snack: Tea Eggs

It is no secret that the Chinese love their tea, but they take tea loving to the next level with one slightly strange snack that you can find right throughout the country. The tea egg is essentially an egg that has been boiled once, the shell is cracked, and then it is boiled again in tea so that the flavour seeps in and so that the outside of the egg white starts to get a beautiful marbled effect from the tea. These are typically cheap and sold by street vendors, so why not give it a try?

51. Go Antiques Shopping at Panjiayuan Market

China is a country with an incredible market culture, and instead of visiting the touristic shops to buy your souvenirs, it can be a great idea to head to local markets where you can find the real deal for a much lower price. Panjiayuan Market is one of our favourite markets for antique items and unique crafts. Whether you want Buddha heads, Chinese porcelain, vintage advertising posters, or calligraphy items, you'll find something to fall head over heels in love with.

52. Be Bowled Over by the Yunhe Rice Terraces

Rice is probably the most important food in all of China, and virtually all of the rice that is eaten on a day to day basis in the country is grown on home soil. This means that there are many stunning rice terraces to be explored around the country, and our favourite of them all might just be the Yunhe Rice Terraces. You'll see pure greenness for miles and miles, and as you walk around and stop into local eateries, you can really get a sense of the local way of life in the Chinese countryside.

53. Have a Day of Learning at the China Science & Technology Museum

While China is a country that is full of history and culture, it's also a country that can be very forward looking and progressive, and this is never more evident than on a trip to the China Science & Technology Museum in Beijing. One building contains items pertaining to ancient Chinese technology, such as astronomy, the compass, gunpowder, and more, and there is another building dedicated to aeronautics, astronautics, energy, and modern science. If you are travelling with kids, this museum is sure to keep them mesmerised.

54. Join in With the Monlam Festival Celebrations

Unfortunately, it's pretty difficult to get into Tibet these days, but whether or not you make it into this region or not, you'll still have the opportunity to find some Tibetan culture. The Monlam Festival is a prayer festival that celebrates the Tibetan New Year, either in February or March. The festival is usually held for around three days, and rituals include traditional Buddhist dance sessions, cake offerings, and prayer sessions. If you can't make it to Tibet, Shangri-La is a good place to experience this.

55. Spot Golden Monkeys in Zhouzhi Nature Reserve

There is an incredible amount of wildlife across China, and one of the best places to spot monkeys is in the Zhouzhi Nature Reserve, a UNESCO Heritage Site. In fact, it's here that 4000 of a rare breed called the Golden Monkey lives. These monkeys are extremely unique to look at because they all have flat, blue faces. You have to trek into the mountains of the park to see these beautiful creatures, but it is 100% worth the effort.

56. Pick Up Some Mandarin

One of the challenges that you are likely to encounter on your trip to China is that not everyone will speak English. In fact, outside of the main cities, hardly anyone will speak English. And this is why it can be a great idea to pick up some basics in Mandarin at the beginning of your trip, even if that can be challenging. We really like the Hutong School in Beijing because it offers classes that are targeted to tourists travelling in China with no prior experience with the language.

57. Visit the First Ever Buddhist Temple in China

If it's history and culture that floats your boat, the White Horse Temple, a little outside of the city of Louyang, is somewhere that you need to visit. This temple is, in fact, the oldest Buddhist temple in all of China, and it dates way back to 64AD, and is extremely well preserved when you consider its age. The Hall of Heavenly Kings, The Hall of the Great Buddha, the Hall of Mahavira, the Hall of Guidance, and the Cool and Clear Terrace all appear in order exactly as they did almost 2000 years ago.

58. Cool Down With a Chinese Style Milk Tea

If you choose to visit China in the summer months, you'll no doubt be searching for every possible to opportunity to cool down a little. Well, when there is no AC in sight and you need to feel a little cooler, we can heartily recommend purchasing a Chinese style milk tea from the streets. Inside you will find plenty of strong black tea that is combined with soya milk, condensed milk for sweetness, and those all important ice cubes that make the drink so refreshing.

59. Have a Fishing Adventure on Taihu Lake

If your idea of the perfect break is sitting on the edge of a lake and calmly waiting for a bite on your fishing rod, you're in luck because China has a number of wonderful fishing locations. Lake Taihu, otherwise known as Lake Tai, is the third largest lake in China, and it has an abundance of freshwater fish in its waters. In the water, you can find white shrimp, whitebait, and white fish, among other varieties.

60. Take a Load Off in Beihai Park

As everyone knows, Beijing is a mega-city. While it's 100% worth visiting on a trip to China, it can also be very overwhelming for some people. But when you are stuck in the city and you are tired of the skyscrapers and cars making noise on the roads, you can find a peaceful oasis in the city at Beihai Park. This former imperial garden was constructed in the 11th century, and it opened as a public park in 1925. With lakes, Chinese flower gardens, and plenty of greenery, it's the perfect place to relax and take in some fresh air.

61. Uncover Ancient History at the Ming Tombs

For tourists who want to get to grips with an important aspect of China's history without walking from museum to museum, the Ming Tombs is a must visit place. The Ming Tombs are the final resting place for 13 of the 16 emperors from the Ming Dynasty. And these are not tombs as you have ever seen them before – each tomb is its own huge temple complex, and the surrounding areas are filled with gigantic animal and human sculptures.

62. Get Cultural at the Macao International Music Festival

While Macao might be best known for its huge casinos, if you are a music fan, Macao is also the place to be during the month of October. This is because this is the time of year when the Macao International Music Festival is held. During this month, musicians from all around the world are invited to Macao to showcase their talents, and a huge variety of music can be found. You'll find chamber concerts, symphonies, operas, classical performances, and more besides.

63. Feel the Serenity of Pudacuo National Park

Located in the Yunnan region of China, the Pudacuo National Park is one of the richest areas in the whole country for biodiversity. The park contains a staggering 20% of all the varieties of plant life that can be found in China, and about one third of the bird and mammal species of the country, including about 100 endangered animal species. You'll also find rare and beautiful orchids, so this is the perfect place to take a load off and enjoy China's incredible natural beauty.

64. Enjoy a Night of Smooth Jazz in Shanghai

When you think of smooth jazz music, China is probably not the first country that pops into your head. But if it's jazz that you want, it's jazz that you shall have and one of the best places to catch a live jazz show is at Long Bar in the Waldorf Astoria in Shanghai. Opulence is the key to every aspect of this bar with incredible art deco design and one of the most comprehensive drinks menus in the city, with over 500 things available for you to choose from. This is somewhere to get dressed up for.

65. Take a Day Trip to Putuoshan Island

If you find yourself in Shanghai with a desire to escape the hustle and bustle of the big city, it can be a great idea to take

yourself on a day trip to Putuoshan Island, one of 1400
islands located at the mouth of Hangzhou Bay. The island is
a breath of fresh air, and is also an extremely important place
for Chinese Buddhism because it is the home of Mount
Putuo, one of four sacred Buddhist mountains in China. Walk
some of the mountain and you will hear the sounds of
Buddhist chanting that emerges from the monasteries.

66. Discover Kazak Customs at Nalati Grasslands

The number of different landscapes you can find in China is
quite staggering, and there are many grasslands around the
country, which offer something different to the mountains
and forests. The Nalati Grasslands are particularly special
because as well as being home to many beautiful meadows
with blooming flowers, these grasslands are also home to the
Kazak minority people in China. It is possible to spend the
night in a Kazak camp and really get to know the local way of
life, which is very much recommended.

67. Indulge a Sweet Tooth With Chinese Mooncakes

While China is a country that is better known for its
scrumptious savoury dishes than its sweet treats, if you do
have a sweet tooth, you should still have no problem finding

something that makes your stomach sing. Chinese Mooncakes are one of the most popular desserts around the country, and while they are mostly eaten during the mid-Autumn Festival, you should find them in good bakeries at any time. Essentially, sweet red bean paste or lotus paste is covered in thin pastry, and it's totally yummy.

68. Cycle the Xi'an Wall

Of course, the most famous wall in China is the Great Wall, but the Xi'an Wall, the wall setting the boundaries for the city of Xi'an, is also very impressive. It is the most complete city wall that has survived in China, and it's also one of the largest ancient military defence systems in the world. The wall is pretty darn huge, and so it's a great idea to rent a bicycle and traverse the wall by putting your foot to the pedal. There are bicycles available for rent at the South Gate.

69. Discover Chinese Acrobatics at Chaoyang Theatre

If you find yourself in Beijing with nothing to do in the evening time, skip the tourist restaurants and take in a show instead. If ballet or opera isn't your thing, we think that you might be more entertained by traditional Chinese acrobatics. The place to catch one of these shows in the city is the Chaoyang Theatre, and the performances are nothing short of spectacular, covering 2000 years of acrobatics history in China.

70. Eat Pumpkin During the Mid-Autumn Festival

The Chinese people love to celebrate, and the Mid-Autumn Festival is one of the most important celebrations of the year, marking, unsurprisingly, the middle of Autumn. As with all festivals in China, eating and drinking is very important, and pumpkin is a food that's really important during this particular festival. Pumpkin represents the bounty of the Autumn harvest, and eating pumpkin symbolically represents the onset of good health.

71. Go Diving on Wuzhizhou Island

While China doesn't exactly have a reputation of being a beach paradise, there are certainly beaches to be found, particularly away from the mainland on China's islands. If you want to find a beach but fancy doing more than lying in the sun, one island in particular is renowned for its diving opportunities. Wuzhizhou Island is a very exclusive part of

China with soft sand and a temperate climate throughout the year. Move into the sea, and you will find coral reefs with sea urchins, sea cucumbers, and plenty of colourful tropical fish.

72. Party All Night at Dada Beijing

As the third largest city in the whole world, Beijing is the kind of place where you can find anything and everything, and if you are a serious party monster, you are in for one hell of a good time in the Chinese capital. There are numerous nightclubs dotted all over the city, but our favourite has to be Dada Beijing. The crowd is mixed, the atmosphere is extremely welcoming, and you can hear multiple genres of different music on any night of the week making it somewhere that anyone can have a good time and dance until the wee hours.

73. Catch a Performance at the Shanghai Spring International Music Festival

China is an incredible country for experiencing a huge variety of cultural activities, and one of the most celebrated cultural events on the Chinese calendar is the Shanghai Spring International Music Festival. This is also one of the longest running contemporary festivals in the country, now running for over 50 years. You'll be able to catch mesmerising classical Chinese music and dance performances from around the world that explore the connections between Chinese culture and foreign countries.

74. Treat Yourself to Green Onion Pancakes From the Streets

When you are on the streets of Shanghai in the mid-afternoon and you want something quick, cheap and tasty to put into your mouth until dinner time, green onion pancakes are the way to go. You might have tried these in Chinese restaurants back at home, abut if you're are not familiar, they are essentially wheat rotis that are filled with the delicious taste of chopped up green onion and served with soy sauce. We can't get enough of them.

75. Walk Through the Steep Cliffs of Longtan Valley

If you are the kind of person who likes to get active on holiday and you want to immerse yourself in China's incredible beauty, Longtan Valley, which is often regarded as the most beautiful valley in the country, is a must visit. Take a trip to this valley and you will find rocky mountains with purple stone, cascading waterfalls, rolling creeks, and tranquil valleys with all kinds of plant life. In short, it's a magical place for nature lovers.

76. Rock Out at the Modern Sky Festival

When you think of the best places in the world for outdoor music festivals, China might not be the first country that comes to mind. But if you find yourself in China in October and you want an excuse to party day and night, you absolutely need to know about the Modern Sky Festival, which is hosted in Beijing every October. While international acts are invited to play at the festival, a strong emphasis is placed on local Chinese bands, so attending this festival is a great way to get to grips with the local music scene.

77. Find Something Special at the Hotan Sunday Market

If you love nothing more than to rummage around for one of a kind items in bustling markets, you will be in shopping heaven in China. The market culture is incredibly strong right around the country, but Hotan Market in Hotan City is a particular favourite of ours. Unbelievably, hundreds of thousands of people visit the market every Sunday, which will give you a sense of its scale. You can find traditional craft items made my minority people, hand woven rugs, exquisite dresses, Chinese porcelain, and of course, lots of food and drink.

78. Discover Buddhist Cave Art in Yungang Caves

China is a place to discover some of the most incredible ancient Buddhist art that exists anywhere in Asia, and one of the most special places for this has to be the Yungang Caves. Across 252 Buddhist cave temples that still exist, you will be able to spot more than 52,000 Buddhist statuettes that date way back to the 5th and 6th centuries. The art work is incredibly well preserved, and through the cave complex, you really get a feel for the artistic genius of ancient Chinese civilisations.

79. Eat Crab Shell Pie on the Streets of Shanghai

As you travel around China, you will notice that there is different street food in every town and city that you visit, and one of the best places for new food discoveries is in Shanghai. A streetside snack that is found on many streets of

Shanghai is called Crab Shell Pie. It is called this because the steamed exterior of the pastry looks like a crab's shell, and inside, you can indeed find minced crab meat, sometimes shrimp too, and the subtle taste of shallot oil as well.

80. Get Artsy With the 798 Art Festival

China is a country that is full of contrasts. There is a huge respect for traditional ways of life, and at the same time it has a booming economy that keeps pushing the country forward in many exciting ways. If you fancy exploring the contemporary arts culture of China, the 798 Art Festival hosted at the end of September every year in Beijing is the festival for you. You will be guided around independent galleries, shops, design studios and more to really get to grips with the current arts scene, and perhaps shop for something special to take home with you.

81. Feel the Speed of the Chinese Grand Prix

If you have the need for speed, the Chinese Grand Prix needs to be on your hit list on a trip to China. Each year, this international racing competition is held at the Shanghai Circuit, which is one of the most celebrated racing tracks in the whole world. In fact, when the race track first opened in

2004, it was the most expensive Formula One circuit in the world, costing $240 million to build.

82. Immerse Yourself in Beauty at the Shanghai Peach Blossom Festival

China is, of course, famed for its natural beauty, but if you have limited amounts of time and you will mostly be visiting the major cities, there is still beauty to be found amongst the huge roads and skyscrapers. We are particularly fond of March and April in Shanghai, because this is when the peach trees start to blossom, and there is even a Shanghai Peach Blossom Festival at this time. Weirdly, part of the festival involves pigs, including pig racing and pig diving. We have no idea why!

83. Buy Really Unique Souvenirs from Shard Box Store

Before you leave China, you will no doubt want to purchase some special souvenirs for your friends, family, and for yourself. There are many tourist stores, but trust us when we say to avoid the tourist traps and head to Shard Box Store in Beijing instead. This shop has an incredibly unique concept.

Basically shards from broken pieces of Ming and Qing Dynasty porcelain that were smashed in the Cultural Revolution, are used to create new boxes, pieces of jewellery, and bottles.

84. Try Some Pickled Cucumber Salad

When you think of Chinese food, you probably think of steamed buns and oodles of chewy noodles, but if you would prefer to chow down on something that is a little bit lighter, we can promise that China won't disappoint, you just have to look at bit harder. A light Chinese food that we absolutely adore is a pickled cucumber salad. This salad is particularly popular in the Sichuan region, and it complements the fiery food of this part of China very well indeed.

85. Dance, Dance, Dance at the Zebra Music Festival

Although China doesn't have a reputation as a country that's great for epic summer festivals, you can definitely find some great music festivals around the country if that floats your boat. One of our favourites is the annual rock and pop festival hosted in Shanghai, which is called Zebra Music

Festival. There are a few international bands on the line-up, but the focus is very much on local acts. And the best thing about it is that the festival is located on Shanghai Beach, so it has a really relaxed coastal atmosphere.

86. Learn About Tea at the China National Tea Museum

While in China, you will soon discover that the local people love nothing more than to sip on a hot cup of tea. But how much do you actually know about this drink? Well, you can find out more at the China National Tea Museum, which is located in Hangzhou. Quite unbelievably, this is the only museum in all of China that is dedicated to tea, and inside you can learn about the growing process, production processes, and the impact of tea on the Chinese culture and economy.

87. Visit Longjing For the Qingming Festival

China is a country that has a huge respect for its history and traditions, and this makes the Qingming Festival, which normally falls on the 4th or 5th of April, one of the most important days of the year. This is the day when respects are paid to ancestors, and it's otherwise known as Tomb Sweeping Day. As you might expect, this festival is a time when locals sweep the graves of loved ones. But fear not, you can join in with the feasting of the day and with the kite flying that also happens.

88. Eat Youtiao, the Chinese Doughnut

What's more comforting than a fluffy doughnut taken straight out of the deep fat fryer? Well, the good news is that virtually every country on the planet has its own version of the humble doughnut, and China is no exception. In China, you'll need to be looking out for something called youtiao. In their appearance, these actually resemble churros, but they are not as crunchy and more light and chewy. Eat them for breakfast dunked in soy milk and you'll be set for the day.

89. Let the Hukou Waterfall Take Your Breath Away

China is a country with vast landscapes, and there are many impressive waterfalls hidden away in the country's natural forests, mountains, and jungles, but perhaps are favourite of them all is the Hukou Waterfall. Located on the Yellow River, this is the second largest waterfall in China, and the only yellow waterfall in the whole world. If you fall in love with this site of natural beauty, it can be a great idea to take a boat tour of the Yellow River to discover more of the area's natural beauty.

90. Have a Meal With a Difference at Trojan Fairy

Beijing is a city that has no shortage of restaurants to choose from, and some restaurants are more, let's say unique, than others. One of the most unique in the city is called Trojan Fairy. The basic premise is that the whole restaurant is pitch black. That's right – you won't be able to see the diners next to you or what you are putting into your mouth. Which is, of course, the whole fun of the place, and it's worth a visit if you want to try something different.

91. Enjoy a Day of Contemporary Art at MOCA

As you stroll around the museums of China, you'll get a sense of the country's history, but what of China's contemporary culture? For that, we totally recommend MOCA in Beijing, the Museum of Contemporary Art. The exhibitions are rotated very regularly so that up and coming artists in China have the chance to showcase their works in a major gallery to the local public and to visiting tourists alike.

92. Wave a Rainbow Flag for Shanghai Pride

While same-sex activity is legal in China, there is no protection for LGBT people in the workplace and there is no gay marriage in the country, and this can make being LGBT in China something of a challenge. To celebrate how far the community has come and to push for further changes in attitude and legal policy, Shanghai Pride is an important date on the LGBT calendar. Shanghai Pride is hosted in June each year, and culminates with a big street parade.

93. Try Tofu Flower Soup For the First Time

If you are the kind of person who avoids tofu on any menu back at home, you definitely haven't tried tofu in China when it is always cooked to perfection and teamed with robust flavours. Tofu flower soup is a really unique dish made with tofu that Beijing residents often like to slurp down for breakfast. Soft tofu is mixed with dried shrimp, seaweed, spices and coriander, which, if you ask us, beats a bowl of boring cereal any day of the week.

94. Go Vintage Shopping at Lolo Love Vintage

If you fancy yourself as something of a fashionista and want to take home some unique threads from your trip to China, you need to get on board with the flourishing vintage scene in increasingly trendy Shanghai. One of our favourite spots for a shop of vintage shopping is called Lolo Love Vintage. This is mostly for the girls, and there is a really awesome selection of retro womenswear with items from China as well as further afield.

95. Hike Through the Yellow Mountains

If you are the kind of person who likes to have incredible outdoor adventures while you are on holiday, China is a country that is not going to disappoint. The most famous mountainous area of China, and a place where you are sure to have some unforgettable hikes, is called the Yellow Mountains. There are strange rock formations, incredible pine forests, and you can even find hot springs, so after a day of strenuous hiking, you can relax your weary muscles.

96. Sip on Rice Wine in Shaoxing

When in China, if you want to make friends with the locals, you have to drink like the locals, and that means sipping on plenty of rice wine. While rice wine can be found in virtually every corner of the country, it's something extra special in the small city of Shaoxing. Shaoxing Old Wine is considered the king of rice wine in China, and anything you buy in this city will be hand crafted with love.

97. Have a Skiing Adventure at Yabuli Ski Resort

China has some incredible mountain landscapes, but you can do more than just look at and take photos of the mountains, you can have adventures on them as well. Whether you are seasoned on the slopes or you would like to try your hand at skiing for the very first time, China is a great place to do so, and one of the most celebrated ski resorts in the country is the Yabuli Ski Resort in Harbin. You can try skiing, snowboarding, and even ski jumping here.

98. Visit Pu'er, a Tea Lover's Paradise

The Chinese do love a cup of tea, and while drinking a cup now and again is a nice way to experience the country's tea culture, there is honestly nothing quite like actually visiting the places in the Chinese mountains where tea is grown.

There are plenty of tea plantations to be found across China, but our favourite place for tea is called Pu'er. This is actually a place that has grown tea for thousands of years, and we promise that a cuppa here will be more than just a little bit special.

99. Rock Til You Drop at the Midi Music Festival

The Midi Music Festival is one of the biggest rock festivals in all of China. If you love nothing more than to rock out in the great outdoors, be sure to etch this festival into your diary for May of each year in Beijing, where it is hosted in one of the city's parks, and attracts thousands upon thousands of attendees. You can discover some Chinese rock acts from around the country, and make new friends based on a shared love of music.

100. Watch a Show at the Oriental Art Centre

Created with the shape of a butterfly orchid that has five petals, the Oriental Art Centre is one of the strangest and most iconic structures in all of Shanghai. It's also a fantastic place to take in an unforgettable cultural performance. The complex contains a performance hall, a concert hall, an opera hall, and an exhibition hall, so you can catch something different on every day of the week at the Oriental Art Centre. Whether you fancy checking out the Shanghai Opera Company or an acrobatics performance, there will be something to make your night in Shanghai one to remember.

101. Learn How to Cook Like a Local in Dali

Yes, the food in China is beyond delicious. But isn't it sad that after leaving China you'll have to go back to the crappy Chinese buffet inside the bus station? Well, if you learn how to cook like a local person that doesn't have to be the case. Of course, there are cooking schools catering to tourists all over the country, but we particularly like Rice and Friends, a cooking school in the perfectly picturesque town of Dali. Their open kitchen on the roof terrace with a view of the mountains is what sold it for us.

Before You Go...

Thanks for reading **101 Coolest Things to Do in China.** We hope that it makes your trip a memorable one!

Keep your eyes peeled on **www.101coolestthings.com**, and have a wonderful trip!

Team 101 Coolest Things

Made in the USA
Lexington, KY
01 October 2016